Why Must I

Take Exercise?

Jackie Gaff

**Photography by
Chris Fairclough**

CHERRYTREE BOOKS

y must I was my unas?

A Cherrytree book

First published in 2005 by
Evans Brothers Ltd
2A Portman Mansions
Chiltern Street
London W1U 6NR

© Evans Brothers Ltd 2005

British Library Cataloguing in Publication Data
Gaff, Jackie
  Why must I take exercise?
  1.Exercise – Juvenile literature 2.Health – Juvenile literature
  I.Title
  613.7'1

ISBN 1-84234312-2

Planned and produced by Discovery Books Ltd
Editor: Helena Attlee
Designers: Ian Winton and Rob Norridge
Illustrator: Joanna Williams
Consultant: Pat Jackson, Professional Officer for School Nursing, The Community Practitioners' and
Health Visitors' Association.

Acknowledgements
The author and publisher would like to thank the following for kind permission to reproduce photographs:
Corbis: p4 (Michael S. Yamashita), p5 (Ariel Skelley), P9 (Joyce Choo), p14 (Gabe Palmer), p15 (Jose Luis
Pelaez, inc./Corbis), p16 (Ron Morsch), p19 (Ariel Skelley), p27 (Jose Luis Pelaez, inc./Corbis), p25 (Troy
Wayrynen/New Sport/Corbis); Getty Images: p7 (Taxi), p28 (Stone).
Commissioned photography by Chris Fairclough.

The author, packager and publisher would like to thank the following people for their participation in
the book: Alice Baldwin-Hay, Heather and William Cooper, Ieuan Crowe and the staff and pupils of
Presteigne Primary School.

Contents

Why must I take exercise?

Exercise is fun. It keeps your body fit and strong, and it can make you feel more cheerful.

If you don't take exercise your body will become unfit, and everything will start to feel like hard work.

Computer games are great – but don't spend all day playing them.

Being fit will make your body strong enough to do everything it was designed to do.

4

When you are fit you can easily run for a bus, pedal your bike up a steep hill, or race down the football pitch to score a goal.

Getting fit now will make your heart and lungs strong. It will help to keep you healthy for the rest of your life.

HEALTHY HINTS

- **Ask your parent or carer if they will walk or cycle to school with you.**

- **Try out a new sport or game.**

- **Do something active every day.**

Try to find a sport that suits you. There is something for everyone.

So keep your body happy – switch off that computer and get moving!

All sorts of exercise

Lots of different things count as exercise, so find something you enjoy.

Here are some ideas for taking exercise: kick a ball around, fly a kite, take the dog for a walk, or put on a favourite CD and dance around your bedroom.

Dogs need exercise every day – and so do you!

Dancing can be a great way to get fit. It makes you more flexible and graceful, too.

- **Always play somewhere safe – in the garden, or with your friends in the park.**

Why not join a **martial arts** class, or start a football or tennis club? It's a great way to make new friends.

Playing tennis will make your arms strong and speed up your **reactions**.

Mighty muscles

Your muscles give you the strength to move. Without them you couldn't even blink your eyes.

Muscles do their job by pulling on bones, skin or other body parts. They tighten to pull, and **relax** to let go.

Muscles can only pull, not push, so they have to work together to get things done.

Mighty mouse

The Romans thought that muscles looked like mice running around under the skin, so they called them *musculi*, or 'little mice'. Over the years, the Romans' *musculi* became our word muscles.

When you smile, 15 different muscles get to work.

When you bend your arm, your **biceps** pulls your forearm towards your shoulder.

When you straighten your arm, another big muscle called the **triceps** pulls it back down again.

Some muscles work in pairs, while others work in teams.

How muscles work

Arm bent

Biceps pulls

Bones

Triceps relaxes

Arm straight

Biceps relaxes

Triceps pulls

For example, about 200 muscles team up every time you take a step.

When you climb a rope the muscles in your arms and legs work hard to pull your body upwards.

Warming up

You must prepare your body for exercise by warming up your muscles.

Warm muscles are more **flexible**, so they are easier to stretch. This makes your body more **supple** all over.

Muscles can be damaged if they are overworked before they are ready. This is called a **strain**, and it makes the muscle sore to touch and painful to use.

Warm up the muscles at the top of your back by stretching both arms out in front of you, with knuckles facing outwards. Press outwards. Do this five times.

Loosen your shoulder muscles by circling your arms, one at a time. Work for a minute on each side.

HEALTHY HINTS

- **Always do some gentle warm-ups before you do any serious exercise.**

Jogging gently on the spot for three minutes is a good way to warm up your muscles.

Warm-up exercises are fun. If you belong to a team or a class, you can do warm-ups together.

Take hold of your left foot and lift it towards your bottom, while pressing your hip forward. Repeat on the other side to warm up the thigh muscles in both legs. Do this five times.

Stretching exercises make your body more supple. This means that you can bend your body more easily.

Try sitting on the floor with your legs stretched straight out in front of you. Can you touch your toes? If not, you should do exercises that help your **joints** to bend easily.

A supple body is much more graceful than a stiff one. Ballet dancers are very supple, and so are gymnasts.

Stretching exercises help your muscles to lengthen and relax. This means that they become more supple.

Try these exercises:

1. On all fours, pull your head and bottom together, so that your back is rounded.

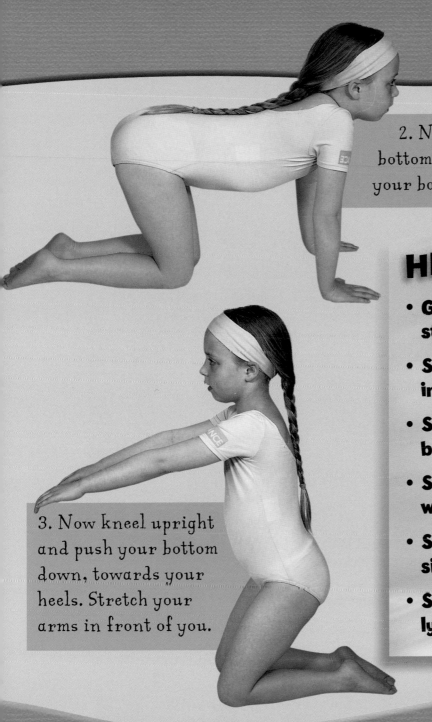

2. Now raise your head and bottom, so that you are stretching your body in the opposite direction.

HEALTHY HINTS

- **Get into the habit of stretching.**

- **Stretch when you get up in the morning.**

- **Stretch after you have been sitting down.**

- **Stretch while you are watching television.**

- **Stretch while you are sitting at the computer.**

- **Stretch when you are lying in bed.**

3. Now kneel upright and push your bottom down, towards your heels. Stretch your arms in front of you.

Tower of strength

Exercise won't give you any new muscles, but working muscles a little harder will build up their strength.

Tennis is a great way to strengthen your arm muscles. Riding your bike will make your leg muscles stronger, and so will cross-country running.

Ice-skating makes your leg muscles stronger.

There are lots of different ways to strengthen your arm muscles.

HEALTHY HINTS

- **If you feel weak or dizzy while you exercise, stop and rest.**

- **Don't punish your body by over-exercising.**

Exercising your muscles is also good for your bones. When muscles move, they put **pressure** on the bones. This pressure makes the bones grow thicker and stronger.

Yoga exercises your muscles and makes your whole body more flexible.

Teaming up

Football, netball and rugby are all team games – they are a great way of taking exercise.

If you don't enjoy the team games you play at school, try something else. What about hockey or volleyball? Find out about new games. There's sure to be something you really enjoy.

As well as helping you to exercise, team games teach you to work with other people.

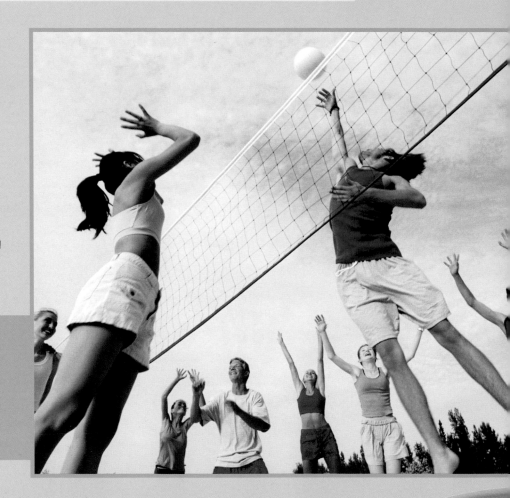

Ancient football

Football was first played in China, about 2,300 years ago. You had to keep the ball in the air, not kick it along the ground!

Whatever game you choose, you will need **stamina** to succeed. Stamina is the strength that keeps you going, allowing you to play your best to the very end of the game. The more exercise you take, the more stamina you will build up.

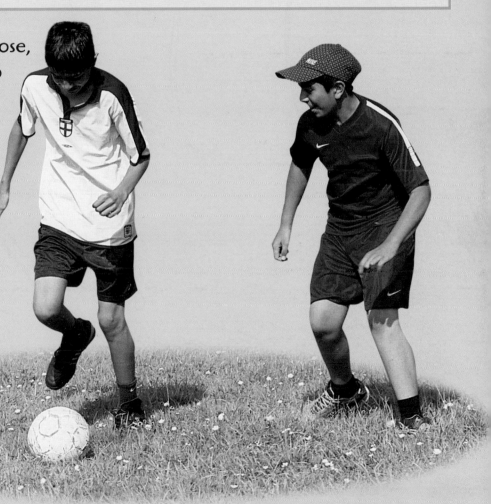

Going solo

If team games aren't for you, don't let that put you off taking exercise.

If you like doing your own thing, but you also want to meet people, why not join a class or club?

If you live close to a lake, a river, or even a swimming pool, you might be able to join a canoe or kayak club.

Ballet develops your muscle-strength and **coordination**.

Paddling a kayak is exciting, and it strengthens your arm, shoulder and chest muscles.

HEALTHY HINTS

- Wear comfortable clothes when you exercise.
- Take an extra layer to put on afterwards.
- Never use a trampoline or go near water without a grown up.

Gymnastics improves your balance, your strength and your overall flexibility.

Try to find out about local sports clubs. Gym classes are an excellent way to exercise.

Taking a deep breat

Whether you're running for a train or racing up and down a swimming pool, hard exercise takes a lot of energy.

Your body gets its energy from the food you eat, but it needs a gas called oxygen to release the energy in the food.

The blood supply

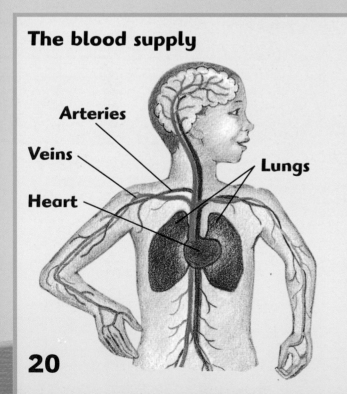

Arteries

Veins

Heart

Lungs

Oxygen is in the air which you breathe into your lungs. It is carried away from your lungs by your blood. The heart muscle pumps this blood all around your body.

This picture shows the blood supply. The **arteries** carry blood away from the heart, and the **veins** carry it back to the heart again.

20

Activities that make your heart and lungs work harder are called **aerobic exercises**.

The more you exercise your lungs, the more air they can pull into your body, and the more exercise you can do.

Your heart gets stronger and healthier with exercise. This means that you are less likely to have problems with your heart when you are older.

When you skip you exercise your heart, as well as your shoulders, arms and legs.

HEALTHY HINTS

- **Try to do some form of aerobic exercise two or three times a week, for twenty to thirty minutes at a time.**

Food and fitness

It's no good doing lots of exercise unless you look after your body in other ways as well.

Your body can't get fit from exercise alone. You need to eat healthy food, too.

Try to avoid food that contains lots of fat, salt or sugar.

After you eat a meal, you should wait at least two hours before starting your exercises. Exercising too soon may give you **cramp**.

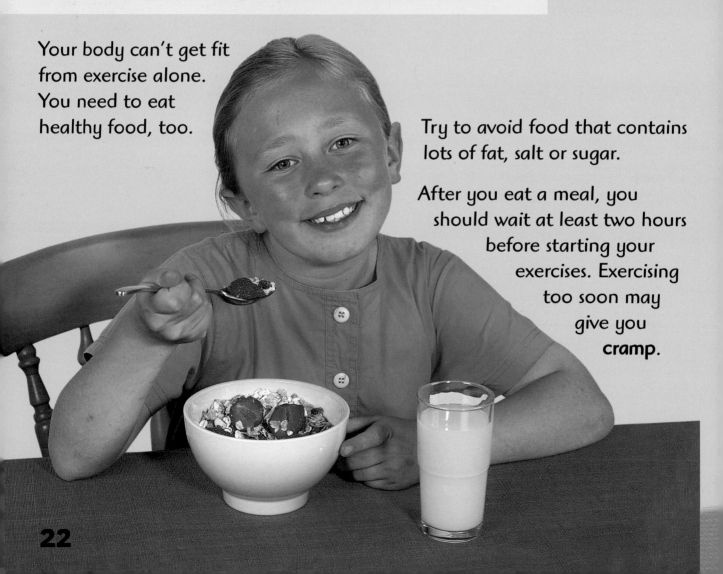

HEALTHY HINTS

- **Sugary foods give you instant energy, but they can make you feel more tired later on.**

- **Take a bottle of water with you.**

- **Drink while you are exercising if you feel thirsty.**

It is important to eat as soon as you can after exercise, but it's no good following up your exercise with a lot of unhealthy, fatty food! A banana sandwich makes an ideal snack.

Sweating during exercise will make you feel very thirsty. Make sure you drink plenty of water, especially if the weather is hot.

If you get hungry, have a light snack – dried fruit or a muesli bar are ideal.

Cooling down

Giving your body time to cool down is just as important as allowing it time to warm up.

Cool-down exercises let your body **temperature, heartbeat** and **breathing rate** slowly get back to normal. They stop you from feeling stiff the next day.

Try to stretch all the muscles that you have been using. Make your movements gradually more gentle.

Stopping exercise too suddenly can send your body into shock. You'll get cold and shivery if you cool down too quickly. You may even feel dizzy and light-headed.

You are bound to feel hot when you finish exercising, but don't forget to put on an extra layer of clothes.

HEALTHY HINTS

- **Spend at least five minutes on your cool-downs.**
- **Put on more clothes so you don't get cold too quickly.**
- **Drink plenty of water after you have finished exercising.**

Athletes always put on a tracksuit after an event.

Exercise should make you feel good, not ill, so give your body a break – treat it to some cool-downs!

Five minutes spent on gentle cool-downs will stop you from feeling stiff later.

Getting your sleep

When you take plenty of exercise, your body will need a good long rest each night.

All your muscles take it easy when you sleep, and your heartbeat and breathing rate slow down. Give your body time to wind down before bedtime.

Reading a book at bedtime will help you relax and drop off to sleep easily.

Try to go to bed at the same time each night. Your body loves this kind of **routine**.

Sleep is when your body builds up a fresh store of energy. If you wake up feeling tired or cross, you're probably not getting enough sleep!

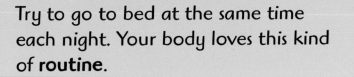

HEALTHY HINTS

- **Make sure you get at least eight hours' sleep each night.**

Stay fit, stay happy

Do you feel tired and lacking in energy some days? Doing nothing won't help!

Exercise really can make you feel better. That's because it kick-starts your body into producing special **chemicals** that make you feel happier.

Sometimes it's easier to exercise with friends.

Exercising and eating healthily are two key steps on the road to a lifetime of feeling fit, happy and fizzing with energy!

HEALTHY HINTS

- Make the most of games time at school.

- Have fun in your free time – do activities you enjoy.

- Do not spend too much time sitting in front of a computer or television.

Glossary

Aerobic exercises
Aerobic exercises are activities that make the heart and lungs work harder to get more oxygen pumping around the body.

Artery
A tube carrying blood from the heart to other parts of the body.

Biceps
The large muscle at the front of your upper arm.

Breathing rate
The speed at which you breathe, pulling air in and out of your lungs.

Chemicals
Chemicals are the substances that make up the world's materials.

Coordination
Ability to make controlled and graceful movements.

Cramp
Cramp is when a muscle goes tight and hard, and really hurts!

Flexible
Flexible means bending easily. Flexible people find it easy to touch their toes, for instance.

Heartbeat
Your heart is a muscle, and like all muscles it moves by tightening and relaxing – this is called its beat, or pulse.

Joint
Joints are places where two bones meet. Some are fixed, but others move – your elbows and knees have moveable joints, for example.

Martial arts
Judo, karate, t'ai chi and tae kwon do are all martial arts, or sports that first grew up in the Far East.

Pressure
Pressure is a pushing force.

Reaction
If you have fast reactions, it means that you move or respond quickly to different situations.

Relax
When a muscle relaxes, it softens and lets go.

Routine
A routine is a regular or set way of doing things.

Stamina
Stamina is another word for staying power – having the energy to keep on exercising, for example.

Strain
A strain is an injury caused by overworking the muscles.

Supple
Supple means able to bend easily. Stretching and bending exercises will help keep your body supple.

Temperature
A measure of how hot or cold something is.

Triceps
The large muscle at the back of your upper arm.

Vein
A tube carrying blood from the body back to the heart.

Further resources

Websites

www.bbc.co.uk/health
BBC website containing articles and news on all aspects of child and adult health.

www.canadianparents.com
A lively website covering all aspects of family life, including health and hygiene.

www.everybody.co.nz
New Zealand's health information website.

www.kidshealth.org
American, child-centred site devoted to all aspects of health and well being. Includes advice on many different aspects of health and exercise.

www.noah-health.org
An American question and answer type site, devoted to all aspects of physical fitness for children.

Books

Barbar's Yoga for Elephants, Laurent de Brunhoff, Harry N. Abrams Inc., 2002.

Body Books – Get a Move On, Anita Ganeri, Evans, 2003.

Bump! Thump! How Do We Jump? Janice Lobb, Kingfisher, 2000.

My Amazing Body: Staying Healthy, Angela Royston, Raintree, 2004.

101 Fun Warm-up and Cool-down Games, John Byl, Human Kinetics Europe Ltd, 2004.

Look After Yourself: Get Some Exercise, Angela Royston, Heinemann Library, 2003.

Index